Ben Franklin
and His First Kite

written by
Stephen Krensky

illustrated by
Bert Dodson

Aladdin

New York   London   Toronto   Sydney   Singapore

First Aladdin edition June 2002

Aladdin Paperbacks

An imprint of Simon & Schuster

Children's Publishing Division

1230 Avenue of the Americas

New York, NY 10020

The text for this book was set in 18 Point Century Old Style.

Designed by Lisa Vega.

The illustrations were rendered in water color.

Manufactured in the United States of America

8 10 9 7

Library of Congress Cataloging-in-Publication Data:

Krensky, Stephen.

Ben Franklin and his first kite / written by Stephen Krensky ;

illustrated by Bert Dodson.–1st Aladdin ed.

p. cm.

Summary: Two popular series, Ready-to-Read and Childhood of Famous Americans, combine
to present the story of young Ben Franklin who loves doing experiments and cannot wait to
test out his latest idea involving a kite!

ISBN-13: 978-0-689-84984-8 (ISBN-10: 0-689-84984-2) (pbk.)

ISBN-13: 978-0-689-84985-5 (ISBN-10: 0-689-84985-0) (library ed.)

[1. Franklin, Benjamin, 1706-1790–Childhood and youth–Juvenile literature.

2. Franklin, Benjamin, 1706-1790–Childhood and youth. 3. Scientists–United States–
Biography–Juvenile literature. 4. Inventors–United States–Biography–Juvenile literature.

5. Scientists. 6. Inventors.]

[E]-dc21

2003273907

Ten-year-old Benjamin Franklin

was hard at work

in his father's candle shop.

He was cutting wicks.

He carefully laid out each one.

Ben stretched his arms
and let out a yawn.
Candles could be tall or short,
fat or thin,
and even different colors.
But there was nothing fun
about candles for Ben.

"When do you think

  we'll be done today?"

Ben asked his father.

"Soon enough," his father answered.

"Why? Do you have special plans?"
Ben's father smiled.
It was a rare day indeed
when Ben did not have
a plan in mind.

"Yes," said Ben.

"I want to try an experiment
at the millpond."

"You'll be swimming, then?"
his father asked.

Ben grinned. "Partly," he said.

His father nodded.

Ben was a fine swimmer.

That afternoon Ben
flew down the streets of Boston.
He was headed for home.
Along the way he noticed the
waves cresting in the harbor.
The ships rocked back and forth.
That was good, he thought.
He needed a strong wind today.

When Ben got to his house,

his mother met him at the door.

Inside, two of his sisters

were busy making

hasty pudding by the hearth.

Ben had sixteen brothers and sisters.

"Ben," his mother said,

"why are you in such a hurry?"

Ben told her about his plan.

"Since your father approves,
I won't keep you,"
said his mother.
"Just be back for supper."
Ben nodded.
He ran to get the kite
he had made the week before.
Then he left the house.

At the millpond
a few of Ben's friends
had arrived to watch.
"You've picked a poor place
to fly a kite," said one.
Ben shrugged.
"I'm doing an experiment," he said.

Ben got undressed.
He gave his clothes
to one of his friends.
"Please carry these
to the other side
of the pond," he said.
"What are you going to do?"
asked the other boys.
"Carry the kite while you swim?"
"No," said Ben.
"The kite is going
to carry me."

"But that kite's nothing special.
It's just paper, sticks, and string,"
said one boy.
"That's true," Ben said.
"But you see,
the kite isn't the invention.
The invention is what
I'm going to do with it."

Ben raised the kite in the air.

Once the wind had caught

and carried it aloft,

Ben walked into the water.

There he lay on his back, floating.

"I'm going to cross this pond
without swimming a stroke,"
said Ben.

The wind tugged on the kite.

The kite string tightened.

The water began

to ripple at Ben's feet.

The kite was pulling him!

The boys whooped
and hollered as Ben
glided across the pond.
Finally he reached the other side.
The other boys met him there.
"That was amazing!" said one.
"You crossed the whole pond
without swimming a stroke,"
said another.

"What will you do next?"

they asked.

"Another invention?"

"A different experiment?"

Ben didn't know.

But he was sure he would think

of something.

This book is based on a story about Benjamin Franklin. The timeline below identifies important events in his life.

1706   Born on January 17, the fifteenth of seventeen children

1716   Goes to work in his father's chandlery at age 10

1718   Becomes apprentice to his brother James

1723   Runs away from Boston for Philadelphia

1729   Buys the *Pennsylvania Gazette*

1730   Marries Deborah Read (has three children)

1732   Begins to print *Poor Richard's Almanack*

1740   Invents Pennsylvania fireplace, later called Franklin Stove

1752   Flies kite in thunderstorm to show that lightning is a form of electricity

1775   Joins the Second Continental Congress

1776   Helps draft and signs the *Declaration of Independence*

1776   Becomes American representative to France

1783   Helps negotiate Treaty of Paris

1790   Dies in Philadelphia on April 17

Ready-to-Read
How many have you read?

Level Two: *Reading Together*

ABE LINCOLN AND THE MUDDY PIG

BE READY AT EIGHT

BEN FRANKLIN AND HIS FIRST KITE

BETSY ROSS AND THE SILVER THIMBLE

BIG BOSS

BUSY WORLD OF RICHARD SCARRY: LOWLY WORM
   JOINS THE CIRCUS

BUSY WORLD OF RICHARD SCARRY: MR. FIXIT'S
   MAGNET MACHINE

CATDOG'S BIG IDEA

CATDOG CATCHER

GRANNY AND THE DESPERADOES

HELEN KELLER AND THE BIG STORM

HENRY AND MUDGE

HENRY AND MUDGE AND ANNIE'S GOOD MOVE

HENRY AND MUDGE AND ANNIE'S PERFECT PET

HENRY AND MUDGE AND THE BEDTIME THUMPS

HENRY AND MUDGE AND THE BEST DAY OF ALL

HENRY AND MUDGE AND THE CAREFUL COUSIN

HENRY AND MUDGE AND THE FOREVER SEA

HENRY AND MUDGE AND THE HAPPY CAT

HENRY AND MUDGE AND THE LONG WEEKEND

HENRY AND MUDGE AND THE SNEAKY CRACKERS

HENRY AND MUDGE AND THE SNOWMAN PLAN

HENRY AND MUDGE AND THE STARRY NIGHT

HENRY AND MUDGE AND THE WILD WIND

HENRY AND MUDGE GET THE COLD SHIVERS

HENRY AND MUDGE IN PUDDLE TROUBLE

HENRY AND MUDGE IN THE FAMILY TREES

HENRY AND MUDGE IN THE GREEN TIME

HENRY AND MUDGE IN THE SPARKLE DAYS

HENRY AND MUDGE TAKE THE BIG TEST

HENRY AND MUDGE UNDER THE YELLOW MOON

IT'S GREAT TO SKATE

MITCHELL IS MOVING

ROMULUS AND REMUS

RUGRATS: BARK, SPIKE, BARK!

RUGRATS: JUNK, SWEET JUNK

RUGRATS: SPACE INVADERS

RUGRATS: STORMY WEATHER

RUGRATS: SURPRISE, ANGELICA!

RUGRATS: TAKE A BOW, BABIES!

SILLY SADIE, SILLY SAMUEL

TITANIC

THE STORY SNAIL

THE TOADY AND DR. MIRACLE

THE WILD THORNBERRY'S: THE BIRD WHO CRIED
   WOLF

THE WILD THORNBERRY'S: DRAWING THE LINE

THE WILD THORNBERRY'S: IN TOO DEEP

THE WILD THORNBERRY'S: SNOWBOUND

WILEY AND THE HAIRY MAN

Level Three: *Reading Alone*

ANIMAL RESCUE

LEAVING VIETNAM

LET'S PLAY CARDS

PEARL HARBOR

PINKY AND REX

PINKY AND REX AND THE BULLY

PINKY AND REX AND THE DOUBLE-DAD WEEKEND

PINKY AND REX AND THE MEAN OLD WITCH

PINKY AND REX AND THE NEW BABY

PINKY AND REX AND THE NEW NEIGHBORS

PINKY AND REX AND THE PERFECT PUMPKIN

PINKY AND REX AND THE SCHOOL PLAY

PINKY AND REX AND THE SPELLING BEE

PINKY AND REX GET MARRIED

PINKY AND REX GO TO CAMP

STRIKING IT RICH

TAKING FLIGHT

Ten-year-old Ben Franklin finds working in his father's candle shop boring—he'd much rather be doing experiments. He can't wait to try out his latest idea. With nothing but a simple kite, can Ben get across the pond—without swimming a single stroke?

Ready-to-Read books offer children a world of possibilities at four different reading levels:

PRE-LEVEL 1 — Recognizing Words

- Word repetition
- Familiar words and phrases
- Simple sentences

LEVEL 1 — Starting to Read

- Simple stories
- Increased vocabulary
- Longer sentences

LEVEL 2 — Reading Independently

- More-complex stories
- Varied sentence structure
- Paragraphs and short chapters

LEVEL 3 — Reading Proficiently

- Rich vocabulary
- More-challenging stories
- Longer chapters

Ready for more? Look for Ready-for-Chapters books.

A Ready-to-Read Book/Nonfiction
ALADDIN PAPERBACKS
Simon & Schuster, New York
Cover illustration copyright © Bert Dodson
Cover designed by Russell Gordon and Lisa Vega
Ages 5–7
www.SimonSaysKids.com
0602

US $3.99 / $5.50 CAN
ISBN-13: 978-0-689-84984-8
ISBN-10: 0-689-84984-2
EAN
9 780689 849848
50399

W8-BAH-050